How to Read a Map

BY LISA M. BOLT SIMONS

The Child's World®
childsworld.com

Published by The Child's World®
1980 Lookout Drive • Mankato, MN 56003-1705
800-599-READ • www.childsworld.com

Photographs ©: Red Line Editorial, cover (map), 7, 9; Evlakhov
Valeriy/Shutterstock Images, cover (compass), 3, 10, 23;
Gagliardi Images/Shutterstock Images, 5; Xi Xin Xing/
iStockphoto, 6; Rob Marmion/Shutterstock Images, 11;
Shutterstock Images, 13, 17 (icons); Albina Glisic/Shutterstock
Images, 14; M. Svetlana/Shutterstock Images, 17 (map); Wave
Break Media/iStockphoto, 18; iStockphoto, 19

ISBN 9781503823280
LCCN 2017944888

Printed in the United States of America
PA02360

ABOUT THE AUTHOR

Lisa M. Bolt Simons is a writer who has published more than 30 books with more on the way. She's also been a teacher for more than 20 years. Her books have been recognized with awards.

Table of Contents

CHAPTER 1

Finding Your Way . . . 4

CHAPTER 2

The Map Legend . . . 8

CHAPTER 3

Directions and the Scale . . . 12

CHAPTER 4

The Grid System . . . 16

Do You Know? . . . 20

Glossary . . . 22

To Learn More . . . 23

Index . . . 24

Answer Key . . . 24

Finding Your Way

Walker is on his way to a birthday party. He has the address, but he doesn't know how to get there. He needs to look at a city map.

Riley is traveling to Uganda with her family. She wants to know what countries are next to Uganda. She needs to look at a world map.

Nathan is at an amusement park. He wants to find his friends at the roller coaster, but he doesn't know where it is. He needs to look at a park map.

There are many kinds of maps. Maps tell you location. They also tell you distance and direction. When you use a map, remember you are looking down. It's as if you are a bird seeing the ground beneath you.

Globes show what the world looks like.

Many of the maps we use are called **reference maps**. Some maps show big areas, such as countries and states. Other maps have details about smaller areas, such as cities. They also include street names.

Maps on buses and trains help people find their stops.

Maps on trains, buses, and subways tell people where the stops are. Buildings, stadiums, and parks have their own maps, too. Knowing how to read a map will help you find your way.

PARTS OF A MAP

Compass Rose

Legend

Scale

Label

Legend

- • City
- ★ Capital
- — Highway
- — Major River
- —·— International Border
- ——— State Border

```
0                    500 Miles
|————————————————————|
0                    500 KM
```

PACIFIC OCEAN

ATLANTIC OCEAN

CANADA

MEXICO

Juneau · Victoria · Seattle · Olympia · Portland · Salem · Vancouver · Spokane · Helena · Boise · Sacramento · San Francisco · Oakland · Carson City · Salt Lake City · Cheyenne · Denver · Santa Fe · Phoenix · Los Angeles · San Diego · Mexicali · Hermosillo · Chihuahua · Edmonton · Calgary · Regina · Winnipeg · Bismarck · Ottawa · Toronto · Montreal · Quebec · Charlottetown · Fredericton · Halifax · Augusta · Montpelier · Concord · Boston · Albany · Hartford · New York · Trenton · Harrisburg · Columbus · Washington D. C. · Richmond · Baltimore · Philadelphia · Norfolk · Charleston · Raleigh · Columbia · Atlanta · Montgomery · Jackson · Baton Rouge · New Orleans · Tallahassee · Jacksonville · Orlando · Tampa · West Palm Beach · Miami

Madison · Lansing · Minneapolis · St. Paul · Des Moines · Lincoln · Topeka · Springfield · Indianapolis · Frankfort · Nashville · Oklahoma City · Little Rock · Memphis · Birmingham · Dallas · Austin · San Antonio · Houston · Chicago · Milwaukee · Detroit · Cleveland · Buffalo · Rochester · St. Louis · Louisville · Kansas City · Omaha · Boulder · Charlotte

Hermosillo · Culiacan · La Paz · Saltillo · Monterrey · Durango · Zacatecas · Ciudad Victoria · San Luis Potosi · Tepic · Leon · Queretaro · Guadalajara · Colima · Mexico City · Toluca · Puebla · Campeche · Merida · Chetumal · Villahermosa · Chilpancingo · Oaxaca · Tuxtla · Belize City · BELIZE

THE BAHAMAS · Nassau · Havana · CUBA · VIRGIN ISLANDS (U.S. & UK.) · DOM. REP. · PUERTO RICO · Port-au-Prince · HAITI · Santo Domingo · JAMAICA · Kingston

The Map Legend

Every map has a legend. A legend is a list of **symbols**. Symbols can be stars, lines, shapes, or pictures. The legend explains the symbols. A common symbol on a map is a star. You'll see on the legend that the star means a capital. Every star you see on the map is a capital. It may be the capital of a state or of a country.

Labels are also used on maps to mark or describe things. Some maps include labels of states or cities. Some maps include labels of natural features such as rivers. Maps that show natural features are called **physical maps**.

Legend

● City

★ Capital

▬ Highway

▬ Major River

▬ ● International Border

▬ ● State Border

Map legends help people find cities and many other features.

Lines on a map may represent roads and boundaries. The size of the line often depends on the size of the road. A line for a county road is usually thinner than a line for a highway. Road names, or **routes**, may also be labeled.

Maps may use shapes as symbols. Some maps have triangles. Triangles may represent mountain ranges. Some maps have rectangles. Rectangles may represent buildings.

Some maps may have pictures as symbols. For example, picnic tables show people where they can eat in a park. Use the legend to figure out each map's symbols. Each map's legend is different.

Country maps might show state borders.

11

Directions and the Scale

A compass rose looks like a star. It shows directions. The four main directions are called cardinal directions. They are north, south, east, and west. Their abbreviations are the first letters of the words: N, S, E, and W.

Sometimes a compass rose has only north, or N. When you look at a map, north is usually on top. Find the compass rose. See where north appears. If north is on the top, south is at the bottom. West is located on the left of the map. East is to the right.

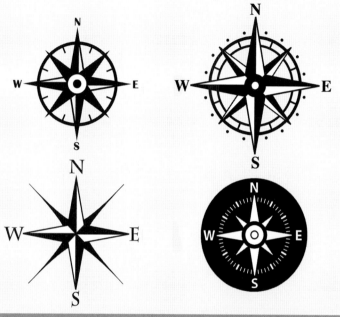

Can you find the directions on these compass roses?

There are four more directions that are halfway between the others. They are called intermediate directions. Northwest, northeast, southwest, and southeast are intermediate directions. Their abbreviations are NW, NE, SW, and SE.

A compass is a device that provides cardinal directions. It helps people find their way when they are lost.

Another feature on a map is a **scale**. A scale tells you the distance on a map compared to the distance in real life. There are different types of scales. One scale might say: "one inch to a mile." This means that one inch on the map is equal to one mile in real life. Sometimes a scale is a line or a bar graph.

Measuring tools will help you use a scale. A ruler or piece of paper will work for straight lines. A scale may say: "one inch to 10 miles." A ruler will help you measure the distance between two places. If it's three inches, then the distance in real life is 30 miles (48 km). If it's six inches, the actual distance is 60 miles (97 km). If you use paper, you can make marks where the scale starts and stops.

The Grid System

Grid systems help people find things. A park, zoo, or town may use maps with grid systems. A grid system is made up of **vertical** and **horizontal** lines. These lines create rows and columns of squares. The squares in the rows may be labeled with capital letters or numbers. The squares in the columns are labeled the opposite. If the rows have letters, the columns have numbers.

Locations on a map with a grid are found with a letter and a number. Let's say you are looking at a town map. The store is at 2F. You go down to row 2. Then you go across to column F. The store is located where the row and the column meet on the same square.

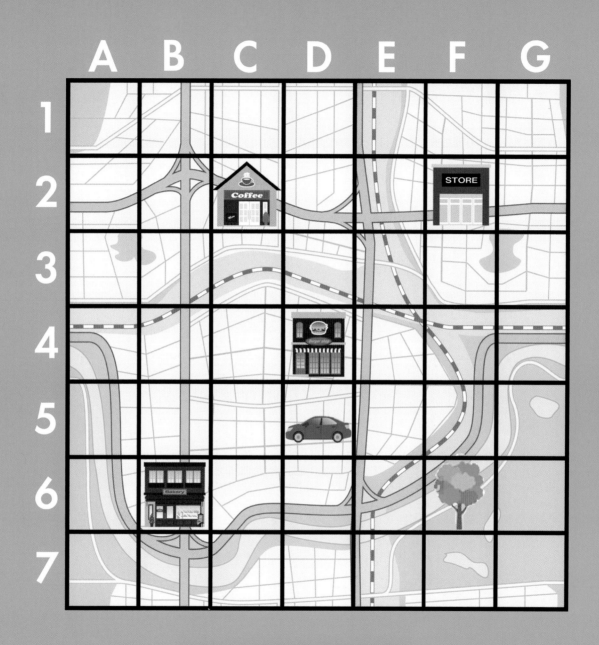

This town map uses a grid system.

Maps help people learn more about the world around them.

Maps come in many shapes and sizes.

All maps help with location, distance, and direction. They can help you find where you need to go. Now you're all set to use a map!

1. Which map feature shows directions?
  A. a scale
  B. a compass rose
  C. a grid system

2. What are the four cardinal directions?

3. What does a star usually stand for on a map?

4. What is the purpose of a legend?
   A. to help measure distance
   B. to show directions
   C. to explain a map's symbols

GLOSSARY

horizontal (hor-uh-ZON-tuhl) Horizontal means going straight across like the horizon. A grid system has horizontal lines.

physical maps (FIZ-uh-kuhl MAPS) Physical maps are maps that show natural features. Some physical maps might show mountains or rivers.

reference maps (REF-uh-renss MAPS) Reference maps are maps that give information about a particular area. City maps are reference maps.

routes (ROWTS) Routes are paths people can use to get from one point to another. Routes are sometimes labeled on maps.

scale (SKAYL) A scale is a tool on a map that helps people measure distances. A scale tells you the distance on the map compared to the distance in real life.

symbols (SIM-buls) Symbols are shapes, letters, or pictures that stand for something real. Many maps use symbols.

vertical (VUR-tuh-kuhl) Vertical means going up and down. A grid system has vertical lines.

TO LEARN MORE

In the Library

Dillemuth, Julie. *Mapping My Day.* Washington, DC: Magination Press, 2017.

Green, Jen. *Mapping a City.* London, England: Wayland, 2016.

Maurer, Tracy Nelson. *Using Road Maps and GPS.* Minneapolis, MN: Lerner Publications, 2017.

On the Web

Visit our Web site for links about how to read maps:
childsworld.com/links

Note to Parents, Teachers, and Librarians: We routinely verify our Web links to make sure they are safe and active sites. So encourage your readers to check them out!

INDEX

compass rose, 7, 12–13

directions, 12–13

grid system, 16–17

legend, 7, 8–10

scale, 7, 15
symbols, 8–10

ANSWER KEY

1. Which map feature shows directions? B. a compass rose

2. **What are the four cardinal directions?** The four cardinal directions are north, south, east, and west.

3. What does a star usually stand for on a map? A star on a map usually stands for a capital city.

4. What is the purpose of a legend? C. to explain a map's symbols